D0646274

Eli and Mort's Epic Adventures
Aspen Snowmass

About this project

The idea for *Eli and Mort's Epic Adventures* Series for kids came from the joy we experienced watching our kids ski, snowboard and have the time of their lives growing up in the mountains. We wanted to share that joy with the world. We decided to write a series of books through the eyes of a child on an epic adventure -- a series of books for adventuring kids like you! *Eli and Mort's Epic Adventures Aspen Snowmass* is the seventh book in the travel, action and adventure Series.

When considering the concept, we imagined what a child might see and feel when they stood at the top of the mountain about to take the first run of the day, and thought, 'Who better qualified to illustrate the book than the children that live here'? As a result, we agreed that the background illustrations should be drawn by the children of the Roaring Fork Valley.

About the characters

Eli, a 5-year-old boy, and his pal Mort the Moose are the best of friends exploring the world together. When others are around Mort is a stuffed moose but to Eli, Mort is his partner in fun. In this book, they experience all that Aspen has to offer.

Eli and Mort are dedicated to the loves of our lives,
Josh, Heath & Will.

Enjoy!

Created by Elyssa and Ken Nager
Published by Resort Books Ltd.
Background illustrations by the children of the Roaring Fork Valley
Character Illustrations by Eduardo Paj
Background cover image by Sarah Teague and Klara Belle Kowar
All rights reserved by Resort Books Ltd. 2016, including the right of reproduction in whole or in part in any form.
Text and illustrations copyright © 2016 by Resort Books Ltd.

Printed in Korea
October 2016

Thank you

We love our friends in Aspen Snowmass. Mort and I think you are AWESOME! Special thanks to Eduardo Paj for making us look so good, Nicole Magistro from the Bookworm who inspired us to write this Series, Brent and Barb Bingham at PhotoFX for digitizing the kids illustrations and Brenda Himelfarb and Diane Pallai for making sure what we wrote was what we meant to write. "Hooray!" to all of the AWESOME children who illustrated this book and their parents for their support.

Special thanks to The Red Brick Council for the Arts for their ongoing support.

Visit **eliandmort.com** to order our latest adventure, check out our events or to just say, "Hi!"

A portion of the proceeds of this book go to The Red Brick Council for the Arts.

The Illustrators

Eli and Mort would like to thank the AMAZING local children, ages 7 to 17, that illustrated the backgrounds! Below are some of their favorite things to do in Aspen Snowmass. What's yours?

D

Chelsea Moore
Aspen High School
15 years old
Favorite: Skiing and exploring the mountains

I

Avery Freedman
Aspen Country Day School
12 years old
Favorite: Skiing Aspen Highlands

A (Left Page)

Sarah Teague
Aspen Community School
14 years old
Favorite: Telemark Skiing, exploring Aspen

E

Amelia Pollack
Aspen Elementary School
7 years old
Favorite: Playing outside and drawing

J

Ava Cherry
Aspen Country Day School
11 years old
Favorite: Skiing and rock climbing

A (Right Page)

Klara Belle Kowar
Aspen Community School
14 years old
Favorite: Skiing and enjoying the wilderness

F

Jozie McConnell
Aspen Middle School
12 years old
Favorite: Skiing, lacrosse, softball and golf

K

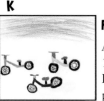

Peter De Wetter
Aspen Middle School
10 years old
Favorite: Skiing, skateboarding, paintball and biking

B

Madeleine Rogers
Aspen Country Day School
12 years old
Favorite: Skiing, horseback riding and shopping in Aspen

G

Jake Doyle
Aspen Country Day School
13 years old
Favorite: Skiing

L

Tyger Campisi
Aspen Community School
12 years old
Favorite: Playing with friends

C

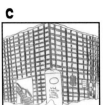

Haver Muss-Nichols
Aspen Community School
10 years old
Favorite: Skiing

H

Macy Hopkinson
Aspen Country Day School
13 years old
Favorite: Skiing

M

Max Schwartz
Aspen Country Day School
11 years old
Favorite: Skiing with friends

N

Kenton Kowar
Aspen Community School
12 years old
Favorite: Skiing, tennis, golf, hockey and snowboarding

T

Finn Johnson
Aspen Community School
10 years old
Favorite: Big mountain skiing

Z

Aurelia Tante
Aspen Elementary School
7 years old
Favorite: Skiing, sledding and ice skating

O

Elizabeth De Wetter
Aspen High School
17 years old
Favorite: Skiing, hiking, biking, going to musical concerts and playing music

U

Maia Dewey
Aspen Country Day School
11 years old
Favorite: Sketching, lacrosse, visiting galleries and snowshoeing

Outtakes

Bennett Jones
Aspen Community School
11 years old
Favorite: Go to Paradise Bakery

P

Sophia Childress
Aspen Middle School
11 years old
Favorite: Go to Paradise Bakery and playing in the fountain

V

Elenor Hicks
Aspen Country Day School
12 years old
Favorite: Skiing, dancing and being outside

Outtakes

Taiga Moore
Aspen Middle School
12 years old
Favorite: Skiing fresh powder

Q

Maya Abraham
Aspen Middle School
13 years old
Favorite: Go to town and watch movies

W

Hannah Popish
Aspen Community School
11 years old
Favorite: Skiing

Outtakes

Mackenzie Kate Triano
Aspen Country Day School
8 years old
Favorite: Figure skating

R

Ethan Ray Uber
Aspen Country Day School
12 years old
Favorite: Play hockey

X

Lindsay Rogers
Colorado Rocky Mountain School
17 years old
Favorite: Adventuring with my friends

Outtakes

Alexander Crete
Aspen Country Day School
12 years old
Favorite: Playing & skiing with my dad

S

Nicole Goth
Aspen Community School
12 years old
Favorite: Eating Paradise Bakery ice cream

Y

Sarah Lyn Teague
Aspen Community School
13 years old
Favorite: Skiing

A is for **Aspen Snowmass**. My dad often told us to, "Shoot for the moon. Even if you miss, you'll land among the stars." When Mort my moose, stepmom, dad, li'l sis and Boo, our new floppy puppy, arrived in Aspen, I said, "Dad, now I know what you mean." We hadn't really reached the moon, but we had landed among the stars in the Shining Mountains of Aspen, Snowmass, Buttermilk and Aspen Highlands. Boo gave a puppy "woof," and our adventure in Aspen began.

B is for **Buttermilk Mountain**. Buttermilk was pretty much built for kids, snowboarders and freestyle skiers who can't wait to do their next trick. Just like Mort and me! As Mort and I hopped on the Summit Express, I said, "Mort I am going to GO BIG today on Bear Jump." Mort said he was going to go even BIGGER!

Madeleine Rogers

C is for the **Creativity** of Shigeru Ban and the people of Aspen. Mr. Ban built Aspen Art Museum partly from paper and cardboard tubes. Mort and I raced each other up the 57 stairs to the top of the museum, which seemed like climbing a mountain. Then we raced back down again. My stepmom yelled, "Slow down!"

What I look like when I really mean it

D is for **Deck**. In Aspen, you can have a picnic in the snow on the mountain! Mort and I sat on the deck and ate the peanut butter and jelly sandwiches that had been squished and warmed up in our pockets while we were skiing. Mort said, "Yum," as he pressed the peanut butter-filled bread on the roof of his mouth to make it stick.

Chelsea Moore

E is for the famous golden **Eagle** at Aspen Center for Environmental Studies. My dad said the eagle was rescued over 30 years ago. Mort and I stared at her and pretended to fly. The eagle stared right back at us. I told Mort that there was magic in her eyes. Mort thought so too.

Amelia P.

F is for **Fort Frog**, the cabin on Buttermilk Mountain that looks just a log building from the Wild West. Mort climbed into the lookout tower and yelled, "Ride 'em cowboy," as I zoomed past, WAY up high on my snowboard.

G is for the **Gong** on the top of Buttermilk Mountain. Mort and I couldn't help ourselves. We had to "gong" it! Goooooooooooong! The noise was so loud, I was sure you could hear it on top of Pyramid Peak. My stepmom told us Pyramid Peak was over 14 thousand feet high. You could see the peak from the top of Buttermilk.

H is for the **Hideout,** where we went to ski school. The school has lots of places where Mort, my li'l sis and I can hide. So when my stepmom and dad came to pick Mort, my li'l sis and me up, it took them a while to find us. Oops!

I is for **Ice Age Trial** on Snowmass where they found the tusk of a mammoth! It was a fossil from the Ice Age, which my dad said took place 100,000 years ago. WHOA! Mort and I imagined giant mammoths skiing through the same trees that we were swooshing and zooming through.

Ice AGE trail

Avery Freedman

J is for the **Jack Rabbit** we met on Buttermilk Mountain. Mort thought he was real, but I told him it was just a costume. I decided that tomorrow I was going to wear my panda bear onesie and ski down the mountain. Mort didn't need a onesie. Neither did Boo. Mort and Boo were fluffy and warm already.

Peter
De Wetter

K is for **Kids** on snow bikes! Mort, my li'l sis and I knew how to ride bikes on the sidewalk, but not on the snow. We said, "Let's shred this," and down the mountain we went. The best part about riding bikes in the snow was that when you fell down in the powder, it didn't hurt at all.

Tyger

WEST BUTTMILK Exp

L is for **Look**. Mort and I decided to take a break when we arrived at the West Buttermilk Express. I said, "Look up Mort," because there was a cloud floating by in the sky that was shaped like a dinosaur. The cloud was white and the sky was the bluest of blue, and beautiful.

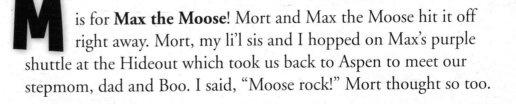

M is for **Max the Moose**! Mort and Max the Moose hit it off right away. Mort, my li'l sis and I hopped on Max's purple shuttle at the Hideout which took us back to Aspen to meet our stepmom, dad and Boo. I said, "Moose rock!" Mort thought so too.

N is for the **Night Sky**. My dad told Mort and me that Aspen was filled with silver, luminaries and movie stars. Mort and I imagined what it must be like to be the man in the moon looking down at the shiny silver and sparkly movie stars. We weren't sure what luminaries were but, hopefully, they were shiny too, so the man in the moon could see them.

O is for Wheeler **Opera House**. Jerome Wheeler was a business man that liked to build stuff like Mort and me. One of the things he built in Aspen was the Wheeler Opera House. And, just like Mort and me, Mr. Wheeler liked stars too, so he painted the ceiling of the Opera House blue, with silver stars.

P is for **Paradise Bakery**. Mort and I liked to sit and talk outside Paradise Bakery and make our teeth freeze, while we ate ice cream. We took one bite of ice cream, and then we took one bite of snow. "That works. My teeth are FROZEN," I said to Mort. Mort agreed. Boo was asleep in the snow.

Q is for Silver **Queen Gondola**. My Dad, Mort and I decided to ride the Silver Queen Gondola to the top of Aspen and back down again. We uploaded, then downloaded. Up the mountain and down the mountain we went. Then we went up the Gondola again to ski back down!

Maya Abrahson

R is for **Restaurant.** Mort and I asked if we could go to The Big Wrap. My stepmom said, "Sure!" She liked The Big Wrap because it was healthy. Mort and I liked it because the wraps were as BIG AS OUR HEADS. I couldn't finish mine. Neither could Mort. But we each still wanted our own wrap anyway.

S is for **Shopping**. The shops in Aspen were FANCY. Mort and I were served fizzy water in special glasses while my stepmom walked around the store. We closed our mouths and let the fizzy bubbles go up our nose until we had to giggle them out.

Nicole G.

T is for **Treehouse Kid's Adventure Center** at the base of Snowmass Mountain. It's a place for kids that looks like a treehouse! My li'l sis decided she wanted to stay at the Treehouse to have some fun while the rest of us skied. That made Mort and me happy, because then we could go even FASTER!

U is for **Ullr Nights** in Snowmass, which is the celebration of the god of snow. The best part of celebrating Ullr was roasting marshmallows. I liked my marshmallows perfectly golden, so I asked my dad to help me. Mort's caught on fire, but Mort liked them that way. Boo sat and begged for more.

V is for the **View** of the Maroon Bells. Mort and I rode a snowmobile from T-Lazy-Z Ranch to the bottom of the Maroon Bells. Zoom - Vroom the snow puffed and fluffed as the snowmobile made its way in the snow. As we looked up, Mort and I imagined ourselves ice climbing to the top of the mountain.

W is for **Wagner Park** where rugby players from around the world come to play. My dad said trees were cut down and dragged by horses to make the goal posts. While we were talking, Mort was busy imagining a dragon drinking lemonade sitting on the cross bar. Sometimes Mort's imagination gets the best of him.

Hannah.

X is for **Xtreme** snow sports. My stepmom said Buttermilk has lots of trails and parks for EXTREME snow sport athletes to GO BIG.

Mort and I dreamed of shredding it in the half-pipe and flying in the air on our snowboards in the slopestyle competition. Woo-hoo!

Y is for yelling **"Yahoo!"** as we zoomed down "Whoa Nelly" sledding hill on our inner tubes at the Aspen Recreation Center. There was so much for kids to do - inside and outside. But Mort and I liked playing outside. Boo bounded around, flopped down and rolled with us down the mountain.

Sarah T.

Z is for **Zoot** the mountain rescue dog. Mort, Boo and I met Zoot as he was riding down the mountain at the end of his work day on a snowmobile. Zoot's job was to keep everyone safe on the mountain. Boo gave Zoot a high-five as he drove by, and our adventure in Aspen came to a dutiful, dogiful end.

Aurelia

Bennett

James

Taiga Moore

Mackenzie

outtakes

There was so much more
to do in Aspen.

See you this Summer
on our next adventure!

Check out our
other adventures
at www.eliandmort.com

Learn to Snowboard

Beaver Creek

Vail

Vail-en Espanol

Breckenridge

Steamboat